SINGING GAMES AND DANCES

Singing Games and Dances

collected and edited by
DAVID S. McINTOSH

ASSOCIATION PRESS • **NEW YORK**

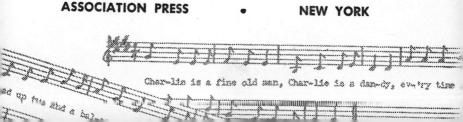

Foreword

The games and dances in this book were selected from material which has been collected in Southern Illinois during the past twenty years. They are all fun to do and they are not difficult. With a strong voice, a good sense of rhythm, plenty of vitality, and adequate preparation, anyone can learn to lead these activities. The tempo should be lively; and to insure this the leader should either play with the group or keep time with his feet, so that he can feel the best speed for the game.

In suggesting an age level for playing these games and dances (see Contents), I have been influenced greatly by observing the reactions of groups which were playing the games and by what I have learned of the traditional use of these materials from talking with people who have participated in them.

In selecting games for use in a particular situation the leader should consider the social development of the participating group; also he should have in mind the social attitudes to be encouraged.

These traditional games and dances provide a great variety of social situations. For instance, games such as "A Tisket, a Tasket" and "Chase the Squirrel" permit individuals to compete with each other; "Draw a Bucket of Water" and "Chicken, My Chicken" demand co-operation; and "Here Goes the Red Bird" and "Rock Candy" permit individuals to demonstrate their ability in dancing. Certain games, such as "Lead Up Two" and "Here Sits a Young Man," are obviously icebreakers and may be used for this purpose in situations where groups are slow in assembling or when they are reluctant to participate.

For the user's convenience this book opens with an explanation of terms related to game or dance formations and to actions and figures in them. It will be noted from the Contents pages that the singing games and dances are arranged by their type of formation—whether single, double or triple circle, singing square, contra, or irregular formation games. Beside each activity is given, in parentheses, the age level suitable for it. At the end of the book is an index arranged alphabetically by titles of songs or games.

So many persons have helped in making this compilation that it is almost impossible to render the thanks that are due. I wish to thank especially those persons whose names appear in these pages with the materials they contributed. My thanks are also extended to many persons whose names do not appear. To those people who have permitted me to participate in their square dances and have been patient with me as I learned, I am deeply grateful.

DAVID S. McINTOSH

Contents

Terms Used

IN FORMATIONS, ACTIONS, AND FIGURES

FORMATIONS

Contra or *Longways:* Two lines of players face each other, the ladies on one side and the gentlemen on the other side opposite their partners.

Double Circle: Partners face counterclockwise, with the ladies on the outside of the circle and the gentlemen on the inside.

Single Circle: All face toward the center; the ladies stand to the right of their partners.

Square Set: Four couples make up each set. Couple one is nearest the source of the music. Couples are numbered to the right around each set.

Triple Circle: In the circle of threes, one gentleman stands between two ladies as all face counterclockwise around the circle.

ACTIONS AND FIGURES

Allemande Left: Gentleman turns to the lady on the left (his corner), lady turns to the gentleman on the right (her corner), they join left hands, turn once around and return to place.

Allemande Right: All dancers give right hands to their partners, turn once around and return to place.

Balance: The gentlemen bow, and the ladies curtsy.

Buzz Step: In the singing game "Hoki Poki" this step is done by each individual alone. The weight is put on the right foot, which is kept in place and raised and lowered as the weight is shifted alternately to the left and right foot while the dancer pushes around with the left foot in a steady rhythm.

Coffee Grind Swing: Couples join hands in skating position with the right hands above the left hands; the lady turns under the arms first, then the gentleman turns under; this turning is continued as the couples move forward around the circle. Both should not turn under the arms at the same time because it is difficult to keep a proper position in the circle and one of the two must keep track of the direction. This action is similar to the childhood stunt of "wringing the dish rag."

Do-Si-Do No. 1: Each gentleman joins his left hand with his partner's and turns her once around, then joins right hand with the opposite lady's and turns her once around; then joins left hand with his partner's and turns her around so that she is standing on his right.

Do-Si-Do No. 2: The gentleman and lady move forward to meet each other, pass each other by the right shoulders, side-step behind each other, then move backward and pass each other by the left shoulder, then move back to original position.

Figure Eight: With the gentleman leading, the first couple, with hands joined, pass between gentleman and lady of couple two, turn to the left, around the lady, pass in front of couple two, turn to the right, make lower loop of the Figure Eight. Then the first gentleman leads his partner between the second couple, turns to the right, around the gentleman, passes in front of couple two, turns to the left, and makes lower loop of the Figure Eight for the second time. When the Figure Eight is completed, the first couple join hands with the second couple and circle once around to the left. The Figure Eight around the third couple is done in the same manner, except that the four members of couples one and two join hands as the first gentleman leads between and around couple three. The Figure Eight around the fourth couple is done in the same manner. In a singing square, such as "London," the Figure Eight around the fourth couple must be done in as small a space as possible so that it can be completed in the time allotted in the song.

Grand Right and Left: Partners face each other and join right hands; gentlemen face counterclockwise and ladies face clockwise, as all move forward; partners drop right hands, join left hands with the next person, join right hands with the next person and so on around the circle.

Grapevine Twist: The group is in the single circle formation, holding hands. The couple opposite the leading couple raises its joined hands, and the leading couple leads under the arch and is followed by all the others. The couple holding up its hands turns under its arms, and everyone moves to the right in a circle facing outward. After one turn, the same couple raises its hands, the leading couple backs through the arch, and the circle is turned right side out.

Once-and-a-Half Swing: This call usually comes after the grand right and left, and indicates that each gentleman should swing his partner once around, then should swing each lady in turn, as all continue to move forward, ladies clockwise, gentlemen counterclockwise, around the set.

Promenade: Couples hold hands, usually in skating position, and march in a counterclockwise direction around the set.

Reel: The reel which is done in the contra formation usually starts after the head couple slide-steps to the foot and back to the head of the formation. The head couple joins right hands and turns once-and-a-half around; then the girl goes to the second boy and the boy to the second girl, and they join left hands and turn around; then the head couple meets in the center and turns by the right hand; next the boy and girl of the head couple go to the third girl and boy and turn by the left, then back in the center by the right and so on down the set.

Swing: This is done in several ways:

1. The usual ballroom dance position may be used. (Partners face each other, join gentleman's left hand with lady's right hand; gentleman places his right hand around the lady's waist, and the lady places her left hand over the gentleman's left shoulder, just below the back of the neck. Partners should stand as far apart as this position will allow, because the two-step is generally used as the couple turns to the left, and there must be as much freedom as possible for the feet to move.

2. Hands may be joined, the gentleman's left hand in the lady's right hand and the gentleman's right hand in the lady's left hand; or, as some people prefer, each grasps the other's arms above the elbows, instead of joining the hands. The turn is always to the left.

Note: The "buzz" step that has become popular in some of the modern square dances does not fit into these traditional games.

Two-Step: This is done to 2/4 meter by stepping forward on the left foot, on the count of one, then sliding the right foot up to the heel and a little to the right of the left foot on the second half of count one, then stepping forward with the left foot on the count of two. For the next measure the step is begun on the right foot, sliding the left, then forward on the right.

Note: This is the basic step used in the traditional singing games and dances of the Middle West. There are many modifications including some heel clicking and toe tapping.

Single Circle Games

ALL 'ROUND THE BRICKYARD

All 'round the brick-yard, re-mem-ber me. I'm goin' to step it,

step it, step it, and a re-mem-ber me.

2. All 'round the brickyard,
   Remember me.
   I'm going to shake it, shake it, shake it,
   And a-remember me.

3. All 'round the brickyard,
   Remember me.
   I'm going to take my loving partner,
   And a-remember me.

4. All 'round the brickyard,
   Remember me.
   I'm going to truck it, truck it, truck it,
   And a-remember me.

5. All 'round the brickyard,
   Remember me.
   I'm going to peck it, peck it, peck it,
   And a-remember me.

FORMATION: Single circle of couples.

ACTION: During the singing of the first two lines of each verse all players march in single file to the left. During the singing of *the last two lines of each verse* the action varies as follows:

Verse 1. Circle stops, and all stamp left foot seven times, in rhythm with the music.

Verse 2. Circle stops, and all place their hands on their own hips and shake their hips seven times, in rhythm with the music.

Verse 3. Circle stops, and partners face each other; girls place both hands on their partners' shoulders, and the boys place both hands on their partners' waists; and each couple dances once around, to the left.

Verse 4. Circle stops, and each dancer places the left hand on the left hip and points with the right hand seven times, in rhythm with the music.

Verse 5. Circle stops, and all dancers nod their heads seven times, in rhythm with the music.

SOURCE: Clara M. Kirk, Marion, Illinois, January, 1948.

ALL 'ROUND THIS WORLD

1. All 'round this world we wan-der, all 'round this world we stray.

2. Some-bo-dy rock-in' my su-gar lump, some-bo-dy rock-in' my su-gar

lump, some-bo-dy rock-in' my su-gar lump, su-gar mo-las-ses too.

3. Oh, you're too slow, my sugar lump,
   Oh, you're too slow, my sugar lump,
   Oh, you're too slow, my sugar lump,
   Sugar molasses too.

4. Get around lively, my sugar lump,
   Get around lively, my sugar lump,
   Get around lively, my sugar lump,
   Sugar molasses too.

5. You've rocked her enough, you'd better give her up,
   You've rocked her enough, you'd better give her up,
   You've rocked her enough, you'd better give her up,
   Sugar molasses too.

6. One more rock and I'll give her up,
   One more rock and I'll give her up,
   One more rock and I'll give her up,
   Sugar molasses too.

FORMATION: Single circle of eight to ten couples, with one couple in the center.

ACTION: During the singing of the first two lines the players in the circle move slowly to the left, while the couple in the center selects a couple and takes them to the center. During the remainder of the song the players in the large circle stand in place.

Verses 3, 4, 5, and 6 are sung to the tune of verse 2. During the singing of all these verses beginning with verse 2, the two couples in the center execute the Do-Si-Do No. 1. This game was obviously created to test the endurance of the players.
At the end of the song the first couple joins the outer circle and the new couple selects another couple, while the group sings the first two lines and moves slowly to the left as was done at the beginning of the game.

SOURCE: Mrs. Opal M. Smith, Jonesboro, Illinois, who learned it from Mr. Clifford Tripp.

BIG-FOOTED FELLER

A big foot-ed fel-ler in a sand-y land, a big foot-ed fel-ler in a

sand-y land, a big foot-ed fel-ler in a sand-y land, all la-dies

fare thee well.

2. Fare thee well, my pretty little Miss,
   Fare thee well, my honey,
   Fare thee well, my pretty little Miss,
   I'll court you again next Sunday.

3. Weavin' and a-rockin' and bound to go,
   Weavin' and a'rockin' and bound to go,
   Weavin' and a'rockin' and bound to go,
   All ladies fare thee well.

4. Jump in the well, my pretty little Miss,
   Jump in the well, my honey,
   Jump in the well, my pretty little Miss,
   I'll fish you out next Sunday.

First Version:

FORMATION: Set of four or five couples.

ACTION: Verse 1. All join hands and circle left.

Verse 2. All do the grand right and left.

Verse 3. Everyone does a two-hand swing all around the circle, beginning with his partner and swinging each one in turn.

Verse 4. All promenade counterclockwise around the circle.

Second Version:

FORMATION: Same as above.

ACTION: First boy goes out and swings the right-hand girl, then the opposite girl, then the girl on the left, then his own partner. All do the allemande left and grand right and left; then all the boys swing their partners; then each girl in turn, all around the ring; and then all promenade around the ring.
Each boy leads out in turn.

SOURCE: Walter Nowland, Scheller, Illinois, 1939.

CAIRO

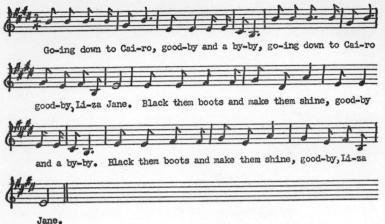

Go-ing down to Cai-ro, good-by and a by-by, go-ing down to Cai-ro

good-by, Li-za Jane. Black them boots and make them shine, good-by

and a by-by. Black them boots and make them shine, good-by, Li-za

Jane.

2. Oh, how I love her, good-by and a by-by,
   Oh, how I love her, I love my Liza Jane.
   I'll be yours if you'll be mine, in the good-by
   and the by-by.
   I'll be yours if you'll be mine, good-by,
   Liza Jane.

8   *Singing Games*

FORMATION: Single circle of not more than ten or twelve couples.

ACTION: Verse 1. During the singing of the first half of the verse, all dance single file, to the left, using the two-step, clog, or stamp dance. The stamp dance is a vigorous stamping of the rhythm with any additional tap beats the dancer can put in.

With the singing of "Black them boots," the gentlemen reverse direction and all do the grand right and left.

Verse 2. During the remaining figures of the dance, the verses or words of the music have no significance except to provide the rhythm, the verses being repeated as often as necessary.

After the grand right and left as partners meet, each gentleman swings each lady once around and when he meets his partner again, he swings each lady twice around. At the end of the swinging, all couples promenade to the end of the verse being sung at the time.

To make the dance more exciting, the leader may shout "Cairo" at any time. At this signal all dancers reverse the direction of whatever figure is being danced and continue in reverse direction until "Cairo" is shouted again.

SOURCE: Mrs. Thad Boston, Centralia, Illinois.

NOTE: There are many versions of this game in the area around Cairo, Illinois, where it originated some time before 1860.

CAME TOO LATE

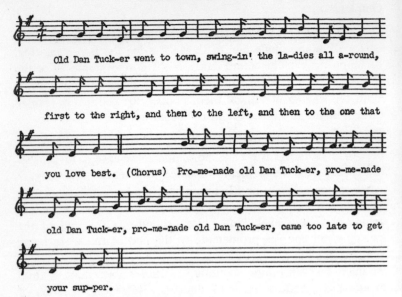

Old Dan Tuck-er went to town, swing-in' the la-dies all a-round,

first to the right, and then to the left, and then to the one that

you love best. (Chorus) Pro-me-nade old Dan Tuck-er, pro-me-nade

old Dan Tuck-er, pro-me-nade old Dan Tuck-er, came too late to get

your sup-per.

FORMATION: Single circle of partners with an extra boy in the center, who is "Old Dan Tucker."

ACTION: During the singing of the verse, "Old Dan" swings as many girls as he can, timing his swinging so as to be with the girl of his choice at the beginning of the chorus.

During the singing of the chorus, all couples promenade and "Old Dan," the boy without a partner, goes to the center of the circle.

SOURCE: Mr. Robert Wilson, Dalgren, Illinois.
Other favorite verses of "Came Too Late":

2. Old Dan Tucker was a man of sense,
   Wore his shirt outside his pants,
   Combed his head with a wagon wheel,
   And died with a toothache in his heel.

3. Old Dan Tucker went to town,
   Ridin' a goat and leadin' a hound,
   The hound would bark and the goat would jump,
   And throw Old Dan a-straddle of a stump.

4. Old Dan Tucker went a-shootin',
   First thing he saw was an old sow a-rootin',
   Head in the hollow and her tail a-shakin',
   Old Dan run to save his bacon.

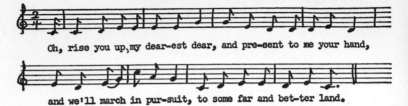

Oh, rise you up, my dear-est dear, and pre-sent to me your hand,

and we'll march in pur-suit, to some far and bet-ter land.

2. Where the boys can reap and mow,
   And the girls can knit and sew,
   And we'll rally round the cane,
   Break and chase the buffalo.

3. And we'll chase the buffalo,
   And we'll chase the buffalo,
   And we'll rally round the cane,
   Break and chase the buffalo.

FORMATION: Single circle of eight to ten couples.

ACTION: Partners face; the gentlemen bow, and the ladies curtsy. All execute the grand right and left around the circle until partners meet; then the gentlemen swing their partners once-and-a-half times and continue in a counterclockwise direction, swinging every lady in turn. When partners meet, they promenade around the circle and back to their starting place. The song is sung over and over again until all the actions are completed. The gentlemen may move to the right and repeat the game with a new partner as often as desired.

SOURCE: Mrs. Phyllis Seelman, Flora, Illinois, May 1, 1952. Mrs. Seelman said, "This game was learned from my grandparents, Mr. and Mrs. Fred Lee of Salem, usually played at lawn parties with forty or fifty people participating."

DEVIL IN THE BANDBOX

1. Devil in the bandbox, can't get him out.

2. Get a twister on him with a long prong stick.

3. Poke him on the north side.

4. Poke him on the high.

5. There he goes, sic him Ti, Yi' Yi' Yi'.

FORMATION: Single circle with the "devil" in the center in a crouching position.

ACTION: All skip in circle around the "devil," while chanting lines one and two.

All move toward the "devil" and perform poking motions on lines three and four.

All move backward into circle formation to give the "devil" room to get through the circle, on "There he goes," and the "devil" starts to run.

All players chase the "devil," starting to run on the last "yi"; the one who catches the "devil" takes his place for the repetition of the game.

SOURCE: Miss Isabel Hall, Collinsville, Illinois, November 1, 1949.

FAR IN THE MOUNTAIN

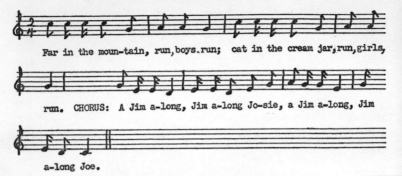

Far in the moun-tain, run, boys, run; cat in the cream jar, run, girls, run. CHORUS: A Jim a-long, Jim a-long Jo-sie, a Jim a-long, Jim a-long Joe.

2. All you girls who want a beau,
   Fall in line with Jim along, Joe.

3. Swing your partner, you know how,
   Grab the one that you love now.

FORMATION: Single circle of four or five couples.

ACTION: Verse 1. The boys run counterclockwise outside of the circle on the words, "Far in the mountain, run, boys, run." The girls run clockwise on the inside of the circle on "Cat in the cream jar, run, girls, run." Partners should meet as the chorus starts.

CHORUS: Every boy swings each girl in turn until he meets his partner. (The chorus is repeated to provide enough time for each boy to swing each girl.)

Verse 2. All march around the circle in the counterclockwise direction. (Indian file.)

CHORUS: The boys hook right elbows with their partners and make a full turn, then they go to each girl and turn by the elbows. The right elbow to their partner, the left elbow to the next girl, and so on.

Verse 3. All swing with their partners, then all swing with their corner.

CHORUS: All promenade with the corner. The game is repeated with the corner lady as the new partner.

SOURCE: Lizzy Simpson, Vienna, Illinois, April 22, 1948, from Mrs. Oscar Pender, Vienna, Illinois, who played the game near Dongola, Illinois, about fifty years ago.

FIRST LADY WALKING

First la-dy walk-ing on the in-side floor, the in-side floor, the

in-side floor. First la-dy walk-ing on the in-side floor, and

bal-ance to your part-ner.

2. Swing your partner and all promenade,
   And all promenade, and all promenade,
   Swing your partner and all promenade,
   And back to your places.

FORMATION: Single circle of not more than eight or ten couples.

ACTION: Any lady may be chosen to be the first lady to walk around inside the circle, as the first verse is sung. (The ladies, as they walk or dance around, have a splendid opportunity to exhibit their charms.) Each lady should time her walk so as to reach her partner and bow or balance, at the end of the first verse.

During the singing of the second verse, each gentleman swings his partner, then all promenade counterclockwise.
After all the ladies have taken their turn, the gentlemen may take their turn in the inside of the circle as the song is changed to "First gent walking on the inside floor."

SOURCE: Mr. Robert Wilson, Dalgren, Illinois.

GO 'ROUND THE MOUNTAIN

Go 'round the moun-tain, to-di-did-dle-um, to-di-did-dle-um.

Go 'round the moun-tain, to-di-did-dle-um, to-di-did-dle-um, dum.

2. Show me your finger . . . .

3. Select your partner . . . .

4. Go through the window . . . .

5. Dance the ball and sing . . . .

FORMATION: Single circle of partners.

ACTION: Verse 1. All two-step (step, close, step) to the left in single file.

Verse 2. All face toward the center of the circle and hold up one finger and shake it in time to the music.

Verse 3. Each boy takes the left hand of his partner in his right hand, and they swing their arms back and forth.

Verse 4. Joined hands are held high, making an arch. On the first four measures the girls go under the arch, and on the last four measures the boys go under the arch.

Verse 5. Partners face each other. The girls place their hands on the boys' shoulders, while the boys place their hands at their partners' waists. They step-hop around, one turn-and-a-half so that the girl is standing on the left of her partner.
As the game is repeated, each boy takes the girl on his right as his new partner.

SOURCE: Leata Ross, who learned it from Mrs. Van Vaitor, Cairo, Illinois.

HERE GOES THE RED BIRD

Here goes the red bird through the win-dow, through the win-dow,

through the win-dow, here goes the red bird through the win-dow,

hi lum did-dle um dee.

2. Take a little girl, go hip-sip-si-da,
   Hip-sip-si-da, hip-sip-si-da.
   Take a little girl, go hip-sip-si-da,
   Hi-lum diddle um-dee.

FORMATION: Single circle of children, hands joined and raised in arches all around the circle. One child is chosen to be It.

ACTION: Circle moves counterclockwise while the child who is It skips in and out, in the clockwise direction, under the raised arms of the other children.

Just as the first verse ends, circle movement stops, It chooses a child from the circle, and they dance in the center of the circle in time to the music.

As the game is repeated the first child joins the circle, and the child that was chosen becomes It. The color of the bird is determined by the color of the clothing worn by the child who is It.

SOURCE: Mrs. Esther Tanner Bush, October, 1946.

HIGHER UP THE CHERRY TREE

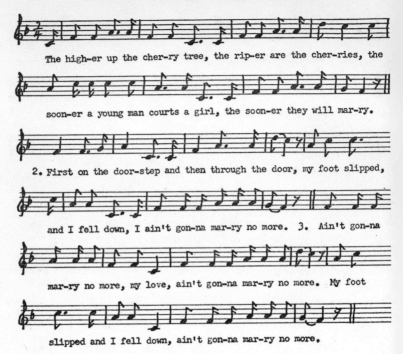

The high-er up the cher-ry tree, the rip-er are the cher-ries, the

soon-er a young man courts a girl, the soon-er they will mar-ry.

2. First on the door-step and then through the door, my foot slipped,

and I fell down, I ain't gon-na mar-ry no more. 3. Ain't gon-na

mar-ry no more, my love, ain't gon-na mar-ry no more. My foot

slipped and I fell down, ain't gon-na mar-ry no more.

FORMATION: Single circle of partners.

ACTION: All circle left while singing the first verse. All execute the grand right and left during the second verse, the boys moving counterclockwise and the girls clockwise. As the verse is ended, each boy chooses the girl whose hand he is holding, and promenades with her during the singing of the last verse.

SOURCE: Alice Mount, Harrisburg, Illinois, 1946.

HOKI POKI

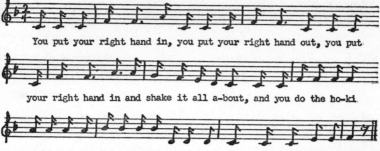

You put your right hand in, you put your right hand out, you put

your right hand in and shake it all a-bout, and you do the ho-ki

po-ki and you do the ho-ki po-ki, and that's what it's all a-bout.

FORMATION: Single circle.

ACTION: Follow the actions of the words on the first four lines, and on the fifth line place left hand on hip, raise right hand high, and shake it in time to the music as you buzz-step around. The game continues with the group singing:

2. You put your left hand in . . . .

3. You put your right foot in . . . .

4. You put your left foot in . . . .

5. You put your right hip in . . . .

6. You put your left hip in . . . .

7. You put your little head in . . . .

and

8. You put your whole self in . . . .

SOURCE: Mrs. Mary Metcalf, Sesser, Illinois, April 4, 1949. This game is an action game that can be played in any formation by any number of players of any age.

I THINK I HEAR THE ANGELS SING

I think I hear the an-gels sing, I think I hear the an-gels sing,

I think I hear the an-gels sing, the an-gels now are on the wing.

I feel, I feel, I feel, that's what my moth-er said, the an-gels

pour-ing 'las-ses down up-on my sleep-ing head. (Chorus) Shoo, fly,

don't both-er me, shoo, fly, don't both-er me, shoo, fly, don't

both-er me, I be-long to com-pa-ny G.

2. If I sleep in the sun, I surely knows,
   If I sleep in the sun, I surely knows,
   If I sleep in the sun, I surely knows,
   A fly comes sting me on the nose.
   I feel, I feel, I feel,
   That's what my mother said,
   Whenever I lays me down to sleep,
   I must cover up my head.

FORMATION: Single circle of couples.

ACTION: Verse 1. During the singing of the first line all join hands and walk four steps to the center raising hands, and during the singing of the second line all return lowering hands. This action is repeated for lines three and four. Beginning with the line "I feel, I feel . . .," all drop hands and face partners, and take the following dance position: each couple with right sides together, the boy's right hand on the girl's left shoulder, the girl's left hand on the boy's right shoulder with other hands clasped, all walk twelve steps, circling around each other. The boy walks under the girl's right arm and turns to his left to face the center of the circle. The girl faces center of the circle. She is now on the left of her original partner.

CHORUS: All promenade. Each boy takes the girl on his right for his new partner.

Verse 2. All repeat the action for the first verse.

CHORUS: All repeat the action for the chorus.

SOURCE: Miss Lyla H. Parker, Mounds, Illinois, 1947.

OLD COW DEAD

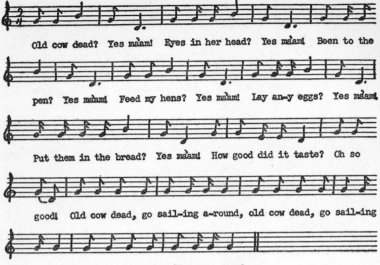

Old cow dead? Yes ma'am! Eyes in her head? Yes ma'am! Been to the pen? Yes ma'am! Feed my hens? Yes ma'am! Lay an-y eggs? Yes ma'am! Put them in the bread? Yes ma'am! How good did it taste? Oh so good! Old cow dead, go sail-ing a-round, old cow dead, go sail-ing a-round, old cow dead go sail-ing a-round.

2. Hey, little girl! Yes, ma'am!
   Been to the picnic? Yes, ma'am!
   See my beau? Yes, ma'am!
   Dance with him? Yes, ma'am!
   Court my beau? Yes, ma'am!
   Kiss my beau? Yes, ma'am!
   How good did it taste? Oh! So good!
   Hey, little girl, go sailing around,
   Hey, little girl, go sailing around,
   Hey, little girl, go sailing around.

3. Hey, little boy! Yes, ma'am!
   Been to the barn? Yes, ma'am!
   See my mare? Yes, ma'am!
   Feed my mare? Yes, ma'am!
   Curry my mare? Yes, ma'am!
   Ride my mare? Yes, ma'am!
   How good did it feel? Oh! So good!
   Hey, little boy, go sailing around,
   Hey, little boy, go sailing around,
   Hey, little boy, go sailing around.

FORMATION: Single circle. One person who is It stands outside the circle.

ACTION: The person chosen to be It does the singing or chanting of the questions and the children in the circle answer "Yes, ma'am" as they dance in the clockwise direction. Each verse begins slowly, and the tempo is gradually increased until at the end of each verse the children are moving very fast.
The game continues until all have had a chance to be It.

SOURCE: Mrs. Josie Rowlett, Cairo, Illinois.

LET'S GO DOWN TO ROWSHA'S

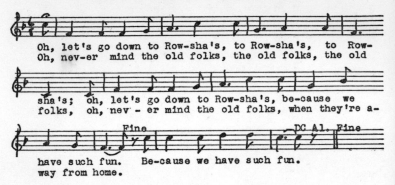

Oh, let's go down to Row-sha's, to Row-sha's, to Row-
Oh, nev-er mind the old folks, the old folks, the old

sha's; oh, let's go down to Row-sha's, be-cause we
folks, oh, nev - er mind the old folks, when they're a-

Fine

have such fun.   Be-cause we have such fun.
way from home.

DC Al. Fine

FORMATION: Single circle of couples, with all holding hands.

ACTION: Verse 1. While singing the first line, all walk toward the
center four steps; on the second line, all walk backward four
steps; on the third line, all walk forward four steps; and on the
fourth line, all walk backward four steps.

As the second "Because we have such fun" is sung, the tempo
is much slower. Partners face each other, join both hands, and
swing arms high toward the center, on "Because"; then swing
arms away from center on "we have"; then swing arms toward
the center on "such fun," and drop hands.

Verse 2. While singing the second verse all do the grand right
and left. When the end of the song is reached, the boy takes for
his partner the girl that he last met in the grand right and left.

SOURCE: Mrs. Mabel Tudor, Rockwood, Illinois, 1945.

ROCK CANDY

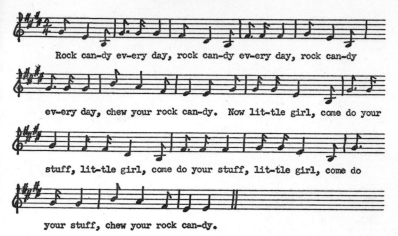

Rock can-dy ev-ery day, rock can-dy ev-ery day, rock can-dy

ev-ery day, chew your rock can-dy. Now lit-tle girl, come do your

stuff, lit-tle girl, come do your stuff, lit-tle girl, come do

your stuff, chew your rock can-dy.

FORMATION: Single circle with one child in the center.

ACTION: All the players in the circle move slowly in a counter-clockwise direction during the singing of the first verse.

During the singing of the second verse the players in the circle stand and pat their feet and clap their hands while the one in the center performs.

At the end of the second verse the one in the center chooses another player, and the game is continued.

NOTE: This game is played merely to "play," or to give vent to one's feelings. The person who is It may do any step he chooses during his turn.

SOURCE: Mrs. Maggie G. Branch, Mounds, Illinois, March 10, 1947.

PIG IN THE PARLOR

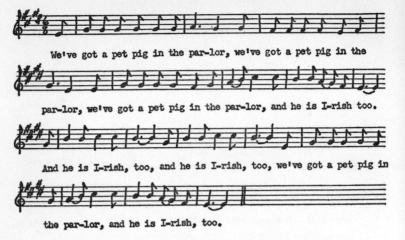

We've got a pet pig in the par-lor, we've got a pet pig in the

par-lor, we've got a pet pig in the par-lor, and he is I-rish too.

And he is I-rish, too, and he is I-rish, too, we've got a pet pig in

the par-lor, and he is I-rish, too.

CHORUS (Sung to the same music as the verse):

> Oh, your right hand to your partner,
> Your left hand to your neighbor,
> Your right hand to your partner,
> And all promenade.
> And all promenade,
> And all promenade,
> Your right hand to your partner,
> And all promenade.

2. Same old pig's in the parlor,
   Same old pig's in the parlor,
   Same old pig's in the parlor,
   And he is Irish, too.
   And he is Irish, too,
   And he is Irish, too,
   Same old pig's in the parlor,
   And he is Irish, too.

3. We've got a new pig in the parlor,
   We've got a new pig in the parlor,
   We've got a new pig in the parlor,
   And he is Irish, too.
   And he is Irish, too,
   And he is Irish, too,
   We've got a new pig in the parlor,
   And he is Irish, too.

FORMATION: Single circle of partners, with an extra man in the center.

ACTION: Verse 1. The players in the circle march around in the counterclockwise direction.

CHORUS: All turn their partners by the right hand, all turn their corners by the left hand, all turn their partners by the right hand, and then all couples promenade. During the turning, the "pig," in the center, tries to get a partner. If he does not get a partner, the players sing the second verse. If he gets a partner, the third verse is sung. The one who is without a partner is the new pig in the center.

The chorus is sung after each verse, and the turning and promenading are repeated. The choice of the verse to be sung is determined by what happens to the "pig."

SOURCE: Essy Racey, Johnson City, Illinois, 1947.

SAILING ON THE OCEAN

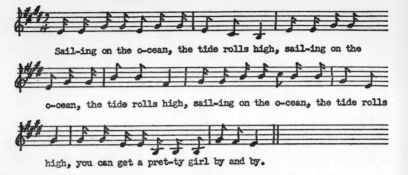

Sail-ing on the o-cean, the tide rolls high, sail-ing on the
o-cean, the tide rolls high, sail-ing on the o-cean, the tide rolls
high, you can get a pret-ty girl by and by.

2. Got me a pretty girl, stay all day,
   Got me a pretty girl, stay all day,
   Got me a pretty girl, stay all day,
   We don't care what the others say.

3. Eight in the boat, and it won't go 'round,
   Eight in the boat, and it won't go 'round,
   Eight in the boat, and it won't go 'round,
   You can leave the pretty girl you just found.

FORMATION: Single circle with four boys in the center.

ACTION: Verse 1. Players in the outside circle join hands and circle clockwise while the boys in the center face toward the outer circle, join hands, and circle counterclockwise.

Verse 2. All players drop hands and both circles walk counterclockwise; each boy in the center chooses from the outside circle the girl who is nearest him, and walks beside her until the end of the verse.

Verse 3. Each boy in the center pulls his partner into the inner circle which moves counterclockwise, while the outer circle moves clockwise. On the word "leave" the boy leaves his partner in the center and goes to the outside circle. The game is repeated with the girls in the center and the words are changed by substituting "handsome boy" for "pretty girl."

SOURCE: Elizabeth Coffman, Anna, Illinois.

SLIPPIN' AND A-SLIDIN'

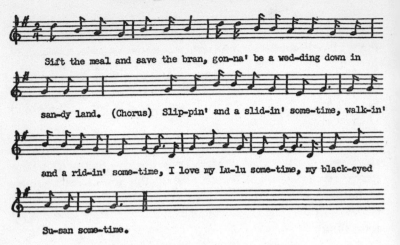

Sift the meal and save the bran, gon-na' be a wed-ding down in

san-dy land. (Chorus) Slip-pin' and a slid-in' some-time, walk-in'

and a rid-in' some-time, I love my Lu-lu some-time, my black-eyed

Su-san some-time.

2. Save your money and buy you a mule,
   Take your girl to Sunday School.

   Chorus:

3. Save your money and buy you a farm,
   Raise sweet potatoes as long as your arm.

   Chorus:

4. Kill a chicken and save the wing,
   Thought I was workin' and I wasn't doin' a thing.

   Chorus:

FORMATION: Single circle of six to ten couples.

ACTION: Verse 1. All circle to the left.

The singing of the chorus is the signal for beginning several figures that follow each other without reference to any particular part of the remaining verses or choruses. This type of tune lends itself to improvising additional verses to fit a local group.

At the beginning of the chorus, each gentleman swings his partner, then swings his corner lady, then all execute the grand right and left. When each gentleman meets his partner, they join either the right or left hands, depending on the number of couples in the dance, walk around each other, and reverse directions for the grand right and left. When partners meet again each gentleman swings his partner; then he goes counterclockwise around the circle and swings each lady in turn until he meets his partner; then all promenade until the end of the verse and chorus being sung at the time. At the end of the promenade, each gentleman turns his partner around so that she is to his left in the circle. As the game is repeated he takes the lady to his right as his new partner.

SOURCE: Mrs. Thelma Whittington, Whittington, Illinois. She said that she played the game when she was a young girl at lawn parties around Whittington.

THAT PRETTY LITTLE GIRL

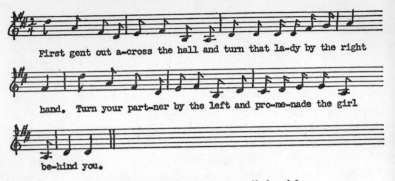

First gent out a-cross the hall and turn that la-dy by the right hand. Turn your part-ner by the left and pro-me-nade the girl be-hind you.

2. Oh, that girl, that pretty little girl,
   The girl I left behind me,
   Every time I think of her,
   The tears flow down and blind me.

Singing Games

FORMATION: Single circle of not more than twelve couples.

ACTION: The first gentleman goes across the circle and turns the opposite lady by the right hand, during the singing of the first two lines; then he and all the gentlemen turn their partners by the left hand, as lines three and four are sung. Each gentleman, as he finishes his turn, leaves his partner and takes up a position to the left of the lady on the left, and all promenade counterclockwise, while the second verse is sung.

As the game is repeated, each gentleman, to the right, leads out in turn.

SOURCE: Mrs. Elsie Parrish McNeill, Carbondale, Illinois.

NOTE: "The words to the second verse were changed occasionally, depending on the originality of the singers. This verse was often sung:

> Oh, that girl, that pretty little girl,
> The girl I left behind me,
> I swapped my wife and a barlow knife,
> For the girl I left behind me."

A TISKET, A TASKET

A tis-ket, a tas-ket, a green and yel-low bas-ket, I sent a let-ter to my love, and on the way I lost it, I lost it, I lost it, and on the way I lost it. I lost it once, I lost it twice, I lost it three times o-ver, a lit-tle boy picked it up and put it in his pock-et.

FORMATION: Single circle.

ACTION: One person, chosen to be It, goes around the outside of the circle carrying either a letter or a handkerchief, which he drops behind someone who picks it up and chases after the one who dropped it. If he catches him before he gets around to the vacant place in the circle, It must go to the center of the circle and become a "rotten egg." If he is not caught, he takes the place of the one who picked up the letter.

Later if the "rotten egg" can steal the letter from behind someone, then that person goes to the center as a "rotten egg."

NOTE: The handkerchief may be dropped at any time during the singing of the song so that the elements of suspense and surprise are a part of the game.

SOURCE: Mrs. Ada L. Fults who learned it from Mrs. Raymond Boswell of Ashley, Illinois.

YOU CAN'T HAVE HER

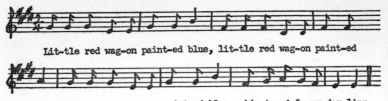

Lit-tle red wag-on paint-ed blue, lit-tle red wag-on paint-ed

blue, lit-tle red wag-on paint-ed blue, skip to m' Lu, my dar-ling.

2. Hairs in the biscuits, two by two,
   Hairs in the biscuits, two by two,
   Hairs in the biscuits, two by two,
   Skip to m'Lu, my darling.

3. Flies in the buttermilk, two by two,
   Flies in the buttermilk, two by two,
   Flies in the buttermilk, two by two,
   Skip to m'Lu, my darling.

4. I'll get another one better than you,
   I'll get another one better than you,
   I'll get another one better than you,
   Skip to m'Lu, my darling.

5. You can't have her, no, no, no,
   You can't have her, no, no, no,
   You can't have her, no, no, no,
   Skip to m'Lu, my darling.

Singing Games

FORMATION: Single circle of partners, with an extra boy in the center. The players in the circle do not join hands.

ACTION: As a verse is sung, the extra boy chooses any girl he wishes and swings her; the girl's partner gets another girl and swings her, and so on. The boy swinging the girl usually starts the verse he wishes to sing. If he wishes to go back and take the same girl he sings, "You can't have her, no, no, no."

SOURCE: Joe Simmons, Vienna, Illinois, 1949.

WHO'LL BE AT THE WEDDING?

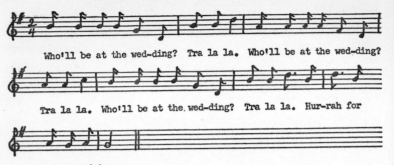

Who'll be at the wed-ding? Tra la la. Who'll be at the wed-ding?

Tra la la. Who'll be at the. wed-ding? Tra la la. Hur-rah for

sug-ar and tea.

2. Miss Sally will be at the wedding, tra-la-la.
   Miss Sally will be at the wedding, tra-la-la.
   Miss Sally will be at the wedding, tra-la-la.
   Hurrah for sugar and tea.

3. Go and choose your lover, tra-la-la.
   Go and choose your lover, tra-la-la.
   Go and choose your lover, tra-la-la.
   Hurrah for sugar and tea.

4. Show your lady motion, tra-la-la.
   Show your lady motion, tra-la-la.
   Show your lady motion, tra-la-la.
   Hurrah for sugar and tea.

5. Show your gentle motion, tra-la-la.
   Show your gentle motion, tra-la-la.
   Show your gentle motion, tra-la-la.
   Hurrah for sugar and tea.

6. Outside the window, tra-la-la.
   Outside the window, tra-la-la.
   Outside the window, tra-la-la.
   Hurrah for sugar and tea.

7. Johnnie, peep at Sally, tra-la-la.
   Johnnie, peep at Sally, tra-la-la.
   Johnnie, peep at Sally, tra-la-la.
   Hurrah for sugar and tea.

8. If you catch her, you may kiss her, tra-la-la.
   If you catch her, you may kiss her, tra-la-la.
   If you catch her, you may kiss her, tra-la-la.
   Hurrah for sugar and tea.

FORMATION: Single circle of partners with one extra girl to start the game.

ACTION: Verse 1. All join hands and dance around to the left.

Verse 2. All raise hands in arches, and Miss Sally goes in and out under the arches, going to the right as the circle moves to the left.

Verse 3. At the beginning of this verse Miss Sally chooses her lover and, holding his hand, she leads him around under the arches as the circle continues to move to the left.

Verse 4. Circle stops moving, Miss Sally and her lover are inside the circle swaying from side to side with considerable movement of the hips. All players in the circle imitate this action.

Verse 5. The action is the same except that the movement of Miss Sally and her lover is changed to a more vigorous swaying. The players in the circle continue to imitate the couple in the center. (Considerable inventiveness is possible on the part of the couple in the choice of movement.)

Verse 6. Miss Sally and her lover dance around the outside of the circle.

Verse 7. Players in the circle raise their hands in arches as Miss Sally goes inside the circle and Johnnie remains outside. They move counterclockwise, peeping around each player in turn until the end of the verse.

Verse 8. Johnnie chases Miss Sally in and out under the arches and, if he catches her, he may kiss her. The chase continues until the end of the verse. If he doesn't catch her, he misses out on the kiss.
Miss Sally selects the next girl to be It as the game is continued. The first names of the players are used when others take the places of Miss Sally and Johnnie.

SOURCE: Mrs. Moneite E. Vaughn, Unity, Illinois, 1947. Additional suggestions for playing the game were obtained from Rosa Belle Bonds, Gates, Tennessee, and Gladys Flewellen, Cairo, Illinois, on July 15, 1952.

Double Circle Games

CAPTAIN JINKS

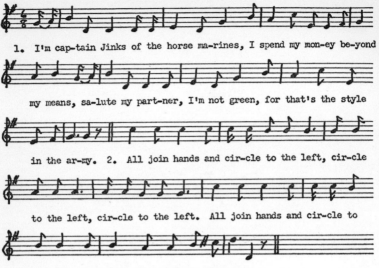

1. I'm cap-tain Jinks of the horse ma-rines, I spend my mon-ey be-yond my means, sa-lute my part-ner, I'm not green, for that's the style in the ar-my. 2. All join hands and cir-cle to the left, cir-cle to the left, cir-cle to the left. All join hands and cir-cle to the left, for that's the style in the ar-my.

3. The captain is the way we fight,
   The gentleman changes to the right,
   Salute my partner, I'm all right,
   For that's the style in the army.

FORMATION: All form a double circle, with the ladies on the outside facing clockwise, and the gentlemen on the inside facing counterclockwise. Each gentleman and lady step back two steps.

ACTION: Verse 1. During the first line of the first verse, all clap hands and take four steps forward, partners passing right shoulders. During the second line, all clap hands and take four steps backward to original position. During the third line, all bow or curtsy to partners. During the fourth line, all turn partners by joining right elbows.

Verse 2. During the singing of the second verse, all join hands in a single circle and walk to the left.

Verse 3 (sung to the tune of the first verse). During the first line of the third verse, all partners bow or curtsy. During the second line, all the gentlemen change to the ladies on the right by passing their partners by the right shoulder. During the third line, all bow or curtsy to the new partners. During the fourth line, all turn new partners by joining right elbows, then take the starting position for the repetition of the game.

SOURCE: Elizabeth Coffman, Anna, Illinois, 1947. She gave the following information about the game: "Mother remembers playing this at a housewarming for one of her older sisters about fifty-five years ago. She said it was played at all the parties and square dances she attended."

GRAB, BOYS, GRAB

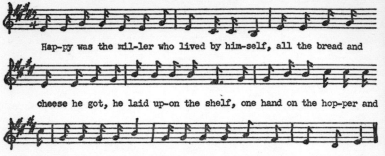

Hap-py was the mil-ler who lived by him-self, all the bread and cheese he got, he laid up-on the shelf, one hand on the hop-per and the oth-er on the slab, ev-'ry time the mill turns, grab, boys, grab.

2. Happy was the miller who lived by himself,
   All the bread and cheese he got, he laid upon the shelf.
   One hand on the hopper and the other on the rack,
   Ladies step forward and the gents step back.

FORMATION: Double circle of partners facing counterclockwise. An extra man is in the center.

ACTION: Verse 1. All promenade until the last word of the first verse is sung, then the boys must grab another partner. It is here that the extra boy has a chance to get a partner.

Verse 2. All promenade during the singing of the first three lines. As the last line is sung, the ladies step forward and the gentlemen step back, so that everyone has a new partner. The extra man may get a partner as this action takes place.

SOURCE: Mrs. Marshall Hopper, Carbondale, Illinois, January, 1941.

A HO JUM JO

The king's in the mid-dle and a ho jum jo, the king's in the mid-dle and a ho jum jo, the king's in the mid-dle and a ho jum jo, and I love my Su-sie Brown.

2. Choose your love as we go 'round,
   Choose your love as we go 'round,
   Choose your love as we go 'round,
   And I love my Susie Brown.

FORMATION: Double circle, facing counterclockwise, with men on the inside. One, two, or three men without partners are in the center.

ACTION: Verse 1. Partners promenade.

Verse 2. At the beginning of the second verse, girls turn in opposite directions, grasp partner's right hand, and everyone does a grand right and left throughout the singing of the verse. While the second verse is being sung, the center player (king, or kings) joins in the grand right and left, thus getting a partner and leaving new ones to be in the center when the game is repeated.

SOURCE: Annamae Todd, Box 482, Pinckneyville, Illinois, April 17, 1951. She said that she learned it from her mother, Mrs. Mary M. Todd of Pinckneyville.

TRIPPING CHARLIE OVER

Char-lie is a fine old man, Char-lie is a dan-dy, ev-'ry time he

goes to town, he buys the la-dies can-dy.

2. Mammy's gone to Shawneetown,
   Daddy's gone to Dover,
   Sister wore her slippers out,
   Tripping Charlie over.

3. Five times five are twenty-five,
   Five times six are thirty,
   Five times seven are thirty-five,
   Five times eight are forty.

4. Five times nine are forty-five,
   Five times ten are fifty,
   Five times eleven are fifty-five,
   Five times twelve are sixty.

FORMATION: All form a double circle of partners, facing in the counterclockwise direction.

ACTION: Verses 1 and 2. All promenade counterclockwise during the singing of the first verse and part of the second verse. On the words, "Tripping Charlie over," all partners swing once around, leaving the gentlemen facing in the clockwise direction, on the inside of the circle, and the ladies facing in the counterclockwise direction, on the outside of the circle.

Verses 3 and 4. While singing verses three and four, the gentlemen march clockwise on the inside of the circle and the ladies march counterclockwise on the outside of the circle, until the words, "Five times twelve," are sung; then each gentleman takes the lady nearest him as his new partner, and the action starts from the beginning as verses one, two, three, and four are repeated.

SOURCE: Mrs. Era Hazel, Centralia, Illinois, 1948. Mr. W. R. Hazel said that the game was played in the vicinity of Dixon Springs about sixty-five years ago.

MILLER'S BIG DOG

The mil-ler's big dog lay on the barn floor and Bin-go was his name. The mil-ler's big dog lay on the barn floor and Bin-go was his name. B - i - n - g - o, B - i - n - g - o, B -- i -- n g -- o, and Bin-go was his name.

FORMATION: Double circle of partners facing in the counter-clockwise direction.

ACTION: All promenade counterclockwise for twelve measures. At measure thirteen, all begin the grand right and left, giving the right hand to partner as the letter "B" is sung, the left hand to the next lady on "I," the right hand to the next lady on "N," the left hand to the next lady on "G," the right hand to the next lady on "O," holding the joined right hands high as the tone is held; and all promenade with these ladies as the final phrase is sung. To vary the game, as the "O" is sung the gentlemen may place their hands at their partners' waists, as the ladies place hands on their partners' shoulders; and the ladies jump as the gentlemen lift.

To vary it another way the couples may embrace as the letter "O" is sung.

SOURCE: Mr. Milo Richman, Cutler, Illinois, 1945.

Triple Circle Games

ALL AROUND

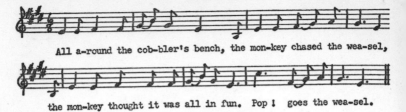

All a-round the cob-bler's bench, the mon-key chased the wea-sel,

the mon-key thought it was all in fun. Pop! goes the wea-sel.

2. All around the baker shop,
   The baker chased the weevil,
   That's where the profit goes,
   Pop! goes the weasel.

3. Five cents a spool of thread,
   Ten cents a needle,
   That's where the money goes,
   Pop! goes the weasel.

4. All around the vinegar jug,
   The monkey chased the weasel,
   The monkey pulled the stopper out,
   Pop! goes the weasel.

5. All around the parlor floor,
   The puppy chased the beetle,
   Around and around the house they go,
   Pop! goes the weasel.

Singing Games

FORMATION: Triple circle facing counterclockwise. The leader numbers the inside person one, the center person two, and the outside person three. Numbers one and three step backward one step and join inside hands, then each gives his free hand to number two.

ACTION: As the song begins, all start marching. When "Pop!" is sung, one and three raise their joined hands and "pop" number two backward under their arms, toward the next couple.

SOURCE: Estella L. Davis, Cobden, Illinois.

GRANDPA DANCE

MUSIC: "Yankee Doodle," "Walking at Night," "John Brown Had a Little Indian," or any good marching tune can be either played or sung.

FORMATION: The players are formed in a large circle of three's with each man, "grandpa," between two ladies, facing in counter-clockwise direction. Several extra men are in the center of the circle.

ACTION: The first half of the tune is sung or played slowly, and each grandpa promenades, with his ladies, in a very dignified manner. During this promenade the extra men may take the places of the promenading grandpas by tapping them on the back. The changing of grandpas continues until the change of tempo in the music.

Now the tune or chorus is played at a fast tempo, and grandpa hooks right elbows with the lady on his right and turns her around, then hooks left elbows with the lady on his left and turns her around, then back to the lady on his right, then again to the lady on his left. If he is lively enough he will finish in time with the music.

The music is again sung or played slowly and the promenade begins as before.

SOURCE: Mrs. Frances Kruell, Sparta, Illinois, December, 1945.

Singing Squares

A BARREL OF 'LASSES

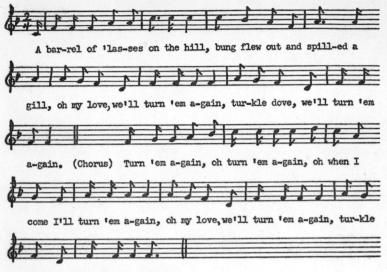

A bar-rel of 'las-ses on the hill, bung flew out and spill-ed a
gill, oh my love, we'll turn 'em a-gain, tur-kle dove, we'll turn 'em
a-gain. (Chorus) Turn 'em a-gain, oh turn 'em a-gain, oh when I
come I'll turn 'em a-gain, oh my love, we'll turn 'em a-gain, tur-kle
dove, we'll turn 'em a-gain.

2. Barrel of 'lasses on the house,
   Bung flew out and shot a mouse,
   Oh my love, we'll turn 'em again,
   Turkle dove, we'll turn 'em again.

3. Barrel of 'lasses on a stump,
   Oh, when I come, oh, let 'em bump,
   Oh my love, we'll turn 'em again.
   Turkle dove, we'll turn 'em again.

4. Barrel of 'lasses, jug of vinegar,
   You can't kiss her, I've done tried her,
   Oh my love, we'll turn 'em again.
   Turkle dove, we'll turn 'em again.

FORMATION: Square set.

ACTION: This song is sung as the dancers execute the square dance figure generally known as the Figure Eight. (See the directions for the Figure Eight under actions and figures.)

SOURCE: Mr. Burton Farley, Vienna, Illinois, 1946.

NOTE: Since the words of this song have no reference to any particular part of the figure, it would not be necessary to sing all the verses. The chorus is to be sung after each verse, and the verses repeated as often as necessary to complete the figure. A tune of this sort provides an opportunity for the leader to improvise words for the first two lines of each verse to fit a local situation.

and Dances

BUFFALO GALS

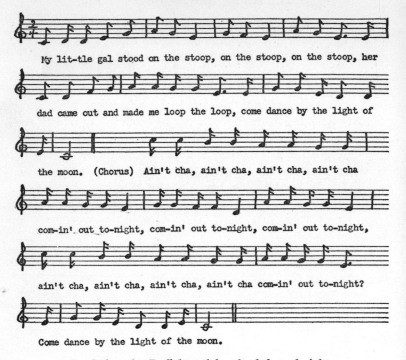

My lit-tle gal stood on the stoop, on the stoop, on the stoop, her
dad came out and made me loop the loop, come dance by the light of
the moon. (Chorus) Ain't cha, ain't cha, ain't cha, ain't cha
com-in' out to-night, com-in' out to-night, com-in' out to-night,
ain't cha, ain't cha, ain't cha, ain't cha com-in' out to-night?

Come dance by the light of the moon.

2. Swing the Buffalo gal by the left and right,
   Left and right, left and right,
   Swing the Buffalo gal by the left and right,
   And dance by the light of the moon.

3. Change the Buffalo gal for another pal,
   Another pal, another pal,
   Change the Buffalo gal for another pal,
   And dance by the light of the moon.

FORMATION: Square set.

ACTION: Verse 1. All promenade in the counterclockwise direction.

CHORUS: Each couple does the Coffee Grind Swing as it moves around the circle in the counterclockwise direction. (See directions for the Coffee Grind Swing under Terms Used in Formations, Actions, and Figures.)

Verse 2. The head couple does the Do-Si-Do No. 1 with couple number two. (See directions for the Do-Si-Do No. 1 under Terms Used in Formations, Actions, and Figures.)

CHORUS: The head couple does the Coffee Grind Swing as it moves counterclockwise around inside the circle, and while the other couples watch.

Verse 3. The man of couple one takes his partner to the couple on his right and exchanges partners, and both couples swing. He then takes girl number two to couple number three and exchanges girl number two for girl number three, and both couples swing. Then he takes girl number three to couple number four and exchanges girl number three for girl number four, and both couples swing.

CHORUS: Each couple does the Coffee Grind Swing as it moves around the circle in the counterclockwise direction.
In repeating the game, the man of couple one leads out again with the girl of couple four for his partner. He leads out in turn with each girl, until he gets his original partner back, then it is time for man number two to lead out.

SOURCE: Maxine Estes, Galatia, Illinois, 1946.

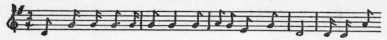

First cou-ple out to Lon-don, and so I heard them say, cou-ple up

four to Lon-don, and so I heard them say.

FORMATION: Square set.

ACTION:

1.
First couple out to London,
So I heard them say,
Couple up four to London,
So I heard them say.

First two couples form a ring and circle to the left.

2.
Do-si-do to London,
So I heard them say,
Do-si-do to London,
So I heard them say.

First two couples do-si-do No. 1. See directions for the Do-Si-Do No. 1 under Terms Used in Formations, Actions, and Figures.

3.
Swing your girl to London,
And so I heard them say,
Couple up four to London,
And so I heard them say.

Each gentleman swings his partner, then the four join hands and circle to the left.

4.
Next couple out to London,
So I heard them say,
'round the lady to London,
And so I heard them say.

Gentleman of the first couple leads, as all four hold fast, and they make a Figure Eight around the lady of couple three.

5.
Back around the gent to London,
So I heard them say,
Couple up six to London,
And so I heard them say.

Gentleman continues and a Figure Eight is made around the man; then the third couple is picked up, and a circle of six is formed.

6.
Balance in to London,
So I heard them say,
Balance back to London,
So I heard them say.

7.
Break and swing your corner too,
So I heard them say,
Right and left to London,
So I heard them say.

8.
Swing the pretty girls to London,
So I heard them say,
Two-hand swing to London,
So I heard them say.

9.
Promenade a ring to London,
So I heard them say,
Promenade a ring to London,
So I heard them say.

10.
Next couple out to London,
So I heard them say,
'round that lady to London,
So I heard them say.

Circle of three couples take four steps into the center and four steps back, then repeat the four steps in and back.

All drop hands, each gentleman turns the left-hand lady by joining left elbows; gives right hand to partner, and continues grand right and left, around the circle. When partners meet, all the gentlemen swing their partners and continue around the circle, swinging each lady in turn, until each meets his partner. All promenade with partner in the counterclockwise direction.

Now the fourth couple is brought into the dance as the action for the fourth verse, with all six holding hands, is repeated.

11.
Cut a Figure Eight to London,
So I heard them say,
Couple up eight to London,
And so I heard them say.

The action for the fifth verse
is repeated.

12.
Balance in to London,
So I heard them say,
Balance back to London,
So I heard them say.

The action for the sixth verse
is repeated.

13.
Break and swing your corners too,
So I heard them say,
Swing your girl to London,
And so I heard them say.

The action for the seventh
verse is repeated.

14.
Swing the pretty girls to London,
So I heard them say,
Two-hand swing to London,
And so I heard them say.

The action for the eighth verse
is repeated.

15.
Promenade a ring to London,
So I heard them say,
Promenade a ring to London,
So I heard them say.

The action for the ninth verse
is repeated.

Now the second couple leads out in the dance as the first verse is changed to "Second couple out to London." After each couple has led out in turn, the dance is finished off with verse sixteen.

16.
Grapevine twist to London,
So I heard them say,
Grapevine twist to London,
So I heard them say.

The circle is turned inside out, by head couple leading across the set to the foot couple and going under their raised arms, as all hold hands.

Verse sixteen is repeated as the foot couple backs through and under the raised arms of the head couple.

SOURCE: Elsie Parrish McNeill and Mrs. Lessie Parrish, Carbondale, Illinois, 1935.

MOLLIE BROOKS

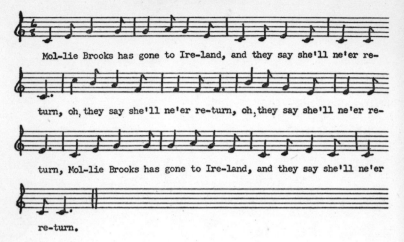

Mol-lie Brooks has gone to Ire-land, and they say she'll ne'er re-

turn, oh, they say she'll ne'er re-turn, oh, they say she'll ne'er re-

turn, Mol-lie Brooks has gone to Ire-land, and they say she'll ne'er

re-turn.

FORMATION: Square, with eight hands joined.

ACTION: Each figure continues just four measures except the last. The song is repeated just once.

Figure 1. All circle-eight clockwise, break into two circles of four, and each group of four—

Figure 2. Circle clockwise, with hands joined, break, and boys join right hands across, girls join right hands across and—

Figure 3. All circle clockwise, break and join left hands across, and—

Figure 4. Circle counterclockwise, break, and join both hands across; boys, whose hands are on top, raise their arms over the heads of the girls, who in turn, raise their arms over the heads of the boys, and with everybody holding fast—

Figure 5. Whirl clockwise for eight measures.

NOTE: If several sets are playing at the same time the players should be numbered in each group of eight from one to eight. The first four would move on to the next group.

SOURCE: Mrs. Mono Jones, Sparta, Illinois, November 14, 1945.

OLD GRAY GOOSE

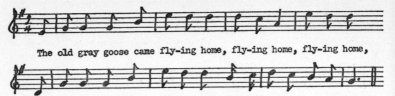

The old gray goose came fly-ing home, fly-ing home, fly-ing home,

the old gray goose came fly-ing home, with a part-ner by her side.

2. Lead up two and balance four,
   Balance four, balance four.
   Lead up two and balance four,
   Swing them four hands round.

3. Round and round and round, and round,
   Round and round and round, and round.
   Round and round and round, and round,
   Swing them four hands round.

FORMATION: Square set.

ACTION: Verse 1. Couples promenade in counterclockwise direction.

Verse 2. The man of the first couple takes his partner by the hand and goes behind couple number two; then passes in front of this couple and forms a circle with them, and they circle to the left.

Verse 3. Each man of couples one and two swings his corner girl while singing the first two lines, and swings his partner while singing the last two lines. And back to—

Verse 1. Couples number one and number two, with number two in the lead, promenade around the set as the first verse is repeated.

Verse 2. The man of the first couple now leads his partner and couple two in a line of four with hands joined, back of couple three and around in front of couple three, and forms a circle of three couples.

Verse 3. Each man swings his corner girl, then his partner. (Couple four is still inactive.) And back to—

Verse 1. Couples number one, two, and three promenade around the set, with number three in the lead, followed by couple two and couple one.

Verse 2. The man of the first couple now leads his partner and couples two and three in a line of six with hands joined, back of couple four, and around in front of couple four, and forms a circle of four couples.

Verse 3. Each man swings his corner girl, then his partner. And back to—

Verse 1. All four couples promenade around the set.
The game is repeated three times so that each couple may act as the lead couple.

SOURCE: Dorotha Greear, Sandoval, Illinois, November 4, 1948.

WAVE HER UP

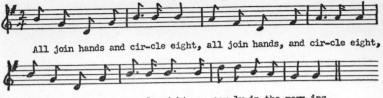

All join hands and cir-cle eight, all join hands, and cir-cle eight,

all join hands and cir-cle eight, so ear-ly in the morn-ing.

2. Knock down Sal and pick up Kate,
   Knock down Sal and pick up Kate,
   Knock down Sal and pick up Kate,
   So early in the morning.

3. Swing your partner like swinging on the gate,
   Swing your partner like swinging on the gate,
   Swing your partner like swinging on the gate,
   So early in the morning.

4. Wave her up and wave her back,
   Wave her up and wave her back,
   Wave her up and wave her back,
   So early in the morning.

5. Wave her down the outside track,
   Wave her down the outside track,
   Wave her down the outside track,
   So early in the morning.

6. Do-si, ladies, do-si-do,
   Do-si, ladies, do-si-do,
   Do-si, ladies, do-si-do,
   So early in the morning.

7. Take them home and get two more,
   Take them home and get two more,
   Take them home and get two more,
   So early in the morning.

FORMATION: Square set.

ACTION: Verse 1. All circle once around to the left.

Verse 2. Each man joins left hands with the lady on his left and turns her around, (Allemande Left), then joins right hands with his partner and does the grand right and left, around the set, until partner is met.

Verse 3. Couples "wring the dishrag" (see explanation in Terms Used in Formations, Actions, and Figures), as they continue to move around the circle, back to the starting position.

Verse 4. Couple one moves to a position facing couple two, and couple two moves apart so as to permit couple one to pass between them. Couple one goes forward between couple two, taking four steps; couple two advances four steps as couple one advances; then both couples walk backward four steps. This action is repeated.

Verse 5. Couple one separates and goes forward on the outside of couple two as couple two moves forward and backward between couple one. The action is the same as for verse four, except for changed positions.

Verse 6. Couples one and two do the Do-Si-Do No. 1 (see directions for the Do-Si-Do No. 1 under Terms Used in Formations, Actions, and Figures).

Verse 7. The two couples circle twice around to the left, couple one leaves couple two, and moves to a position in front of couple three. Couple one repeats the action of verses four, five, six, and seven with couple three and then moves on to couple four, again repeating the actions of verses four, five, six, and seven. Couple one returns to its former position in the circle, and the game is repeated, starting at verse two. When verse four is reached, couple two leads out and follows the routine set by couple one.

and Dances

The game or dance is continued until all couples have gone through all the action.

SOURCE: Cecil Fulkerson, Raum, Illinois, 1946.

WHOA THERE, MULE

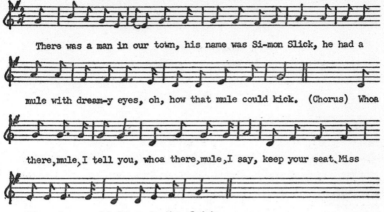

There was a man in our town, his name was Si-mon Slick, he had a
mule with dream-y eyes, oh, how that mule could kick. (Chorus) Whoa
there, mule, I tell you, whoa there, mule, I say, keep your seat, Miss
Li-za Jane, and hold on to the sleigh.

1. There was a man in our town,
   His name was Simon Slick,
   He had a mule with dreamy eyes,
   Oh, how that mule could kick!

   CHORUS:
   Whoa there mule I tell you,
   Whoa there mule I say,
   Keep your seat, Miss Liza Jane,
   And hold on to that sleigh.

2. Sleigh bells am a-ringin',
   Snow am fallin' fast,
   Got the harness on this mule,
   And got him hitched at last.

3. Liza is a dandy,
   Liza is a pearl,
   Liza is the cutest thing,
   Liza is my girl.

4. See this mule a-flyin',
   Take care, watch him sail,
   Watch his ears a-floppin',
   And watch him shake his tail.

5. Goin' down to the parson's,
   Now, Liza, you keep cool,
   Ain't got time to kiss you now,
   I'm busy with this mule.

FORMATION: Square set.

ACTION: Verse 1. Lines 1 and 2, all circle to the left, on line 3 all circle halfway back, and on line 4 all balance. (See directions for the balance under Terms Used in Formations, Actions, and Figures.)

Chorus. All promenade counterclockwise.

Verse 2. All the gentlemen go to the center and circle to the left as the ladies circle to the right.

Chorus. All join hands with partners and promenade counterclockwise.

Verse 3. On lines 1 and 2 all the gentlemen do-si-do with the corner lady and on lines 3 and 4 they do-si-do with their partner. This is the Do-Si-Do No. 2 (see directions under Terms Used in Formations, Actions, and Figures).

Chorus. All promenade.

Verse 4. All the gentlemen swing the corner lady during the singing of lines 1 and 2, and they swing their partners on lines 3 and 4.

Chorus. All promenade.

Verse 5. All "roll the barrel and roll the barrel again." (Couples three and four make an arch with their hands, and couples one and two dance under the raised arms of couples three and four; then turn under their own arms; couples one and two make the arches and couples three and four dance under the raised arms of couples one and two, then they turn under their own arms.)

Chorus. All stand in place and clap their hands as they sing.
In repeating the dance, the gentlemen should change partners with the gentlemen to the left.

SOURCE: Leota McFadin, Carterville, Illinois, January 8, 1948.

WHILE YOUR DEAR REMINDS YOU

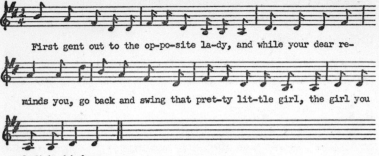

First gent out to the op-po-site la-dy, and while your dear re-

minds you, go back and swing that pret-ty lit-tle girl, the girl you

left be-hind you.

2. Same gent out to the right-hand lady,
   And while your dear reminds you,
   Go back and swing that pretty little girl,
   The girl you left behind you.

3. Same gent out to the left-hand lady,
   And while your dear reminds you,
   Go back and swing that pretty little girl,
   The girl you left behind you.

4. The jaybird right and the yellowhammer left,
   And while your dear reminds you,
   Go back and swing that pretty little girl,
   The girl you left behind you.

5. Once-and-a-half as we go by,
   And while your dear reminds you,
   Go back and swing that pretty little girl,
   The girl you left behind you.

6. And if ever I pass this road again,
   And the Indians they don't find me,
   I'll stop a while and see my girl,
   The girl I left behind me.

FORMATION: Square set.

ACTION: Verses 1, 2, and 3. The first gentleman swings the opposite girl, then his own, then the right-hand girl, then his own, then the left-hand girl, then his own.

Verse 4. All players execute the grand right and left until partners meet.

Verse 5. All swing once around; each gentleman swings each girl in turn until he gets back to his partner.

Verse 6. All promenade around the set.

SOURCE: Mr. and Mrs. John Golder, Carlyle, Illinois, May 6, 1947.

Contra Games

BOSTON GIRLS

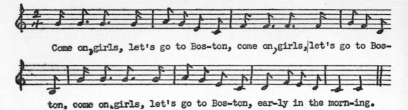

Come on, girls, let's go to Bos-ton, come on, girls, let's go to Bos-
ton, come on, girls, let's go to Bos-ton, ear-ly in the morn-ing.

2. Come on, boys, let's go to Boston,
   Come on, boys, let's go to Boston,
   Come on, boys, let's go to Boston,
   Early in the morning.

3. Oh, Johnny, I'll tell your daddy,
   Oh, Johnny, I'll tell your daddy,
   Oh, Johnny, I'll tell your daddy,
   How you go a-courting.

4. Twice a week, and all day Sunday,
   Twice a week, and all day Sunday,
   Twice a week, and all day Sunday,
   How you go a-courting.

FORMATION: Contra, with six ladies on one side and six gentlemen on the other.

ACTION: Verse 1. All the ladies join hands and all the gentlemen join hands. As the first verse is sung, the two gentlemen at each end of the line of gentlemen raise their joined hands high in an arch. The head lady leads her line under the arch formed by the two head gentlemen; then the line of ladies continues on behind the line of gentlemen and goes under the arch formed at the foot of the line of gentlemen.

Verse 2. The action is reversed for this verse. The two head ladies and two foot ladies form arches and the gentlemen go through and back to their starting position.

Verses 3 and 4. The head couple walks down and up and down between the lines, as if strolling down a shady lane in the moonlight. At the end of the fourth verse they take their places in line at the foot.

The game may be repeated until all couples have strolled, and the original couple is back at the head of the line.

SOURCE: Mrs. Mono Jones, Sparta, Illinois, 1945.

CHASE THE SQUIRREL

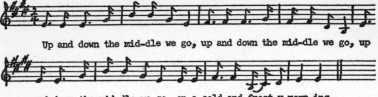

Up and down the mid-dle we go, up and down the mid-dle we go, up

and down the mid-dle we go, on a cold and frost-y morn-ing.

2. Up and down and around we go,
   Up and down and around we go,
   Up and down and around we go,
   On a cold and frosty morning.

3. Catch that squirrel if you can,
   Catch that squirrel if you can,
   Catch that squirrel if you can,
   On a cold and frosty morning.

4. A little faster if you please,
   A little faster if you please,
   A little faster if you please,
   On a cold and frosty morning.

FORMATION: Contra, with seven to ten girls on one side and the same number of boys on the other side.

ACTION: Verse 1. Head couple promenades down the center and back.

Verse 2. Head couple separates, each going behind its own line to the foot.

Verse 3. The boy chases the girl. If the boy fails to catch the girl during the singing of verse three, the fourth verse is used.
When the girl is caught, or at the end of the fourth verse, the active couple go to the foot of the set.
The girls in the line may help the girl who is being chased by holding hands and preventing the boy from breaking through, and the boys may do the same for the boy so the girl cannot break through.

SOURCE: Mrs. Anna Stevenson, Sparta, Illinois, 1945.

GOING TO THE PARTY

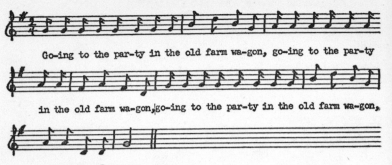

Go-ing to the par-ty in the old farm wa-gon, go-ing to the par-ty

in the old farm wa-gon, go-ing to the par-ty in the old farm wa-gon,

get up, dap-ple grey.

2. One spring's broke and the other one saggin',
   One spring's broke and the other one saggin',
   One spring's broke and the other one saggin',
   Get up, dapple grey.

3. One wheel's off, and another one's saggin',
   One wheel's off, and another one's saggin',
   One wheel's off, and another one's saggin',
   Get up, dapple grey.

4. Fill up the bed with straw in the bottom,
   Fill up the bed with straw in the bottom,
   Fill up the bed with straw in the bottom,
   Get up, dapple grey.

5. Come on, my beauties, go a-trottin',
   Come on, my beauties, go a-trottin',
   Come on, my beauties, go a-trottin',
   Get up, dapple grey.

6. All the way home without upsettin',
   All the way home without upsettin',
   All the way home without upsettin',
   Get up, dapple grey.

Singing Games

7. Good-by girls, I'm glad I met you,
    Good-by girls, I'm glad I met you,
    Good-by girls, I'm glad I met you,
    Get up, dapple grey.

FORMATION: Five or six couples in contra formation with the men in one line and the ladies in the other.

ACTION: Verse 1. The head couple join hands and slide-step down the center to the foot and back to the head of the set.

Verse 2. The head couple reels as in the "Virginia Reel."

Verse 3. The reeling continues.

Verse 4. The reeling continues.

Verses 5 and 6. When the head couple reaches the foot of the set, everyone joins hands in promenade position facing toward foot of set; and the head couple leads the set in a circle of couples back to the head of the set, then to the foot of the set and back to the head of the set.

Verse 7. The partners now separate, the ladies moving down one line and the gentlemen moving down a line opposite that of the ladies, so that the set is reformed as it was in the beginning, except that the head couple has become the foot couple and couple number two has become the head couple.

SOURCE: Miss M. Fulton, Sparta, Illinois, December, 1945.

MICHIGAN GIRLS

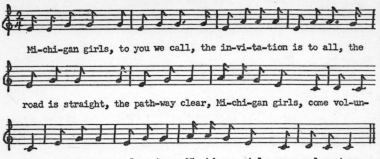

Mi-chi-gan girls, to you we call, the in-vi-ta-tion is to all, the

road is straight, the path-way clear, Mi-chi-gan girls, come vol-un-

teer, vol-un-teer, vol-un-teer, Mi-chi-gan girls, come vol-un-teer.

FORMATION: Contra set of six or seven couples.

ACTION: In this game the action proceeds without regard to any part of the verse. We use the names of different states to add variety to the song such as Illinois girls, or Indiana girls.

Head girl and foot boy go forward and bow, then back to place. Action repeated by head boy and foot girl.

Head girl and foot boy go forward and pass back-to-back (Do-si-do No. 2). Action repeated by head boy and foot girl.

Head girl and foot boy clasp right hands and move around each other. Action repeated by head boy and foot girl.

Head girl and foot boy clasp left hands and move around each other. Action repeated by head boy and foot girl.

Head couple join both hands and slide down to the foot and back to place, then "reel" to the foot of the set. (See explanation of "Reel" in Terms Used in Formations, Actions, and Figures.) At the end of the reel, the head couple slide-steps back to the head. All make an arch, and head couple goes through the arch to the foot and forms an arch, each couple following and making an arch as soon as it passes through. This requires the line to keep shifting toward the head. When the head couple gets back to head position it again passes through, leaving a new head couple (couple number two), the original head couple becoming the foot couple.

Action is repeated until all have acted as head couple.

SOURCE: Mrs. Rubert Maxwell, Sparta, Illinois, November, 1945.

OVER THE MEADOW

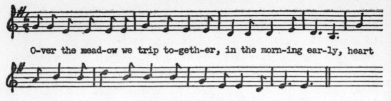

O-ver the mead-ow we trip to-geth-er, in the morn-ing ear-ly, heart

to heart and hand to hand, 'tis true I love you dear-ly.

2. Want no more of your weevily wheat,
   Want no more of your barley,
   Take some more of your good old rye,
   To bake a cake for Charley.

3. Charley, he's a nice young man,
   Charley, he's a dandy.
   Charley likes to kiss the girls,
   Whenever it comes handy.

4. Five times five are twenty-five,
   Six times five are thirty,
   Seven times five are thirty-five,
   Eight times five are forty.

5. Nine times five or forty-five,
   Ten times five are fifty,
   Eleven times five are fifty-five,
   Twelve times five are sixty.

6. Over, over,
   Ten times over,
   Take your pardner by the hands
   And wring the dish rag over.

FORMATION: Contra set of six to eight couples. Boys are in one line and the girls are in the other line.

ACTION: The head couple slide-steps down the center and back to the head of the set, then the head couple executes the reel. (See explanation in Terms Used in Formations, Actions, and Figures.) The head couple should time the speed of the reel so as to reach the foot of the set at the end of verse five.

During the singing of verse six, they "wring the dishrag" three times, then take their places at the foot of the set. The action for "wringing the dishrag" is the same as for the "Coffee Grind Swing," except that partners turn under their arms at the same time. (See explanation in Terms Used in Formations, Actions, and Figures.) The game is repeated from the beginning for the other couples in the set.

SOURCE: Mr. and Mrs. John Golder, Carlyle, Illinois, May 6, 1947.

WAY DOWN IN THE PAW-PAW PATCH

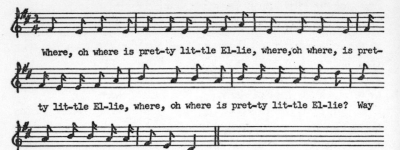

Where, oh where is pret-ty lit-tle El-lie, where, oh where, is pret-

ty lit-tle El-lie, where, oh where is pret-ty lit-tle El-lie? Way

down yon-der in the paw-paw patch.

2. Pickin' up paw-paws, put 'em in a basket,
   Pickin' up paw-paws, put 'em in a basket,
   Pickin' up paw-paws, put 'em in a basket,
   Way down in the paw-paw patch.

3. Here she comes and I'll go with her,
   Here she comes and I'll go with her,
   Here she comes and I'll go with her,
   Way down in the paw-paw patch.

4. Swing a lady up and down, swing a lady home,
   Swing a lady up and down, swing a lady home,
   Swing a lady up and down, swing a lady home,
   Way down in the paw-paw patch.

FORMATION: Four couples make a set, and any number of sets may join in the dance. Partners stand in longways formation, facing each other.

ACTION: Verse 1. The head couple walks down and back between the lines, looking for Ellie.

Verse 2. The head couple walks down and back again, and stoops to "pick up paw-paws and put 'em in a basket."

Verse 3. The head couple faces down the set, joins inside hands, and walks down the center, crosses over, and walks back outside the opposite line to partner's original position.

Verse 4. The head gentleman goes to second lady; they link right arms and turn around. He then does the same with the third lady and with the fourth lady. The head lady does the same down the line of gentlemen. On the last line of the verse, the head couple swings and goes to the foot of the set.
The second gentleman and lady become the head couple and the dance goes on.

SOURCE: Audrey Lee Farris, Crossville, Illinois, March 30, 1949.

WHERE, OH WHERE?

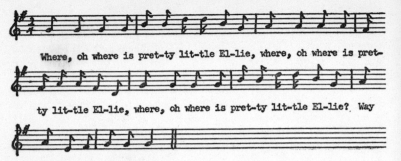

Where, oh where is pret-ty lit-tle El-lie, where, oh where is pret-ty lit-tle El-lie, where, oh where is pret-ty lit-tle El-lie? Way down in the paw-paw patch.

2. Pickin' up paw-paws, puttin' 'em in the basket,
   Pickin' up paw-paws, puttin' 'em in the basket,
   Pickin' up paw-paws, puttin' 'em in the basket,
   Way down yonder in the paw-paw patch.

3. Here she comes and I'll go with her,
   Here she comes and I'll go with her,
   Here she comes and I'll go with her,
   Way down yonder in the paw-paw patch.

FORMATION: Contra with the girls in one line and the boys in the other.

ACTION: Verse 1. All the couples join hands, forming an arch through which the girl of the head couple disappears while the group sings "Where, oh where . . .," and comes back to place by going around the girls.

Verse 2. Ellie goes down through the arch again pretending to pick up paw-paws and put them in a basket, coming back around the boys just in time for her partner to find her.

Verse 3. The head couple join hands and go down through the arch and stay at the foot of the set.
The game is repeated with a new head couple.

SOURCE: Mrs. Virginia Simpson, Barnhill, Illinois, January 15, 1953. Mrs. Simpson said that the game was played by young adults near Burnt Prairie, Illinois, about sixty years ago, and the impression was recalled by Flora Quindry Simpson that the arch represented paw-paw trees and served to conceal Ellie as well as giving the impression of "Way down yonder." Burnt Prairie was first called Liberty, Illinois, and is older than Chicago.

Irregular Formation Games

CHICKEN, MY CHICKEN

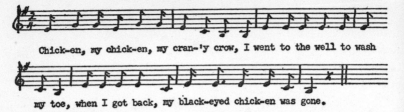

Chick-en, my chick-en, my cran-'y crow, I went to the well to wash my toe, when I got back, my black-eyed chick-en was gone.

Old Mother Hen:
    Chicken, my chicken, my cran'y crow,
    I went to the well to wash my toe,
    When I got back, my black-eyed chicken was gone.

Chickens:	What time is it, old witch?
Witch:	One o'clock.
Chickens:	What time is it, old witch?
Witch:	Two o'clock.
Chickens:	What time is it, old witch?
Witch:	Three o'clock.
Witch:	I want a chicken.
Chickens:	Can't have one.
Witch:	I must have a chicken.
Chickens:	Shan't have one.

FORMATION: A line of twelve children, each standing behind the other. The one at the head of the line is Mother Hen. All the children in line clasp their hands around the waist of the child in front. One extra child who is to be the old witch, stands several feet in front of the line, facing Mother Hen.

ACTION: All stand still as the mother hen sings and during the dialogue. At the end of the dialogue the old witch tries to get past the outstretched arms of the mother hen to touch one of the chickens lined up behind. The line of the mother hen and the chickens must hold fast and be alert to move to prevent the old witch getting past the mother hen. The old witch must get past the mother hen without being touched by her. Sometimes the old witch cannot catch a chicken, so some other child is chosen to be the old witch. If a chicken is caught the old witch takes him to her house, where he must stay while the old witch tries to catch another chicken. Sometimes it is a good idea for a different old witch and mother hen to be chosen each time the game is repeated.

Another way of playing the game is as follows:

FORMATION: Single circle of fifteen to twenty children with one extra child in the center who is the old witch. One of the children in the circle is chosen to be the mother hen, all the other children are chickens.

ACTION: As the mother hen sings the tune, she and the chickens in the circle join hands and move to the left. At the end of the singing all the children drop hands and stand in place as the dialogue is carried on between the old witch and the chickens. At the end of the dialogue, the witch chases the chickens and catches as many as she can. The ones she catches are bewitched, and they help catch the other chickens as the game is repeated until all are caught. In the repetition the chickens that are bewitched stand with the witch in the center of the circle.

SOURCE: Portia Cross, Carmi, Illinois, April, 1949.

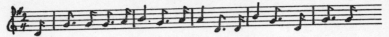

Here comes a duke a rid–ing, a rid–ing, a rid–ing, here comes a

duke a rid–ing, ran–son, tran–son, ti e i oh.

Duke: Here comes a duke a-riding, a-riding, a-riding,
Here comes a duke a-riding, ranson, transon, ti-e-i-oh.

Group: What are you riding here for, here for, here for,
What are you riding here for, ranson, transon, ti-e-i-oh.

Duke: I'm riding here to get married, married, married,
I'm riding here to get married, ranson, transon, ti-e-i-oh.

Group: Well, who do you think you'll marry, marry, marry,
Well, who do you think you'll marry, ranson, transon
ti-e-i-oh.

Duke: I'm going to marry   ,   , (Names some girl),
I'm going to marry   ,   , ranson, transon, ti-e-i-oh.

Group: You're too black and dirty, dirty, dirty,
You're too black and dirty, ranson, transon, ti-e-i-oh.

Duke turns with back toward the group and sings:
I'm no dirtier than you are, you are, you are,
I'm no dirtier than you are, ranson, transon, ti-e-i-oh.

Group: How do you think you'll get her, get her, get her,
How do you think you'll get her, ranson, transon, ti-e-i-oh?

Duke: I'll walk right up and take her, take her, take her,
I'll walk right up and take her, ranson, transon, ti-e-i-oh.

The duke asks the girl, "Will you come?"
She says, "No!"

Duke: You little rascal, you wouldn't come, wouldn't come,
          wouldn't come,
          You little rascal, you wouldn't come, ranson, transon,
          ti-e-i-oh.

The duke asks her, "Will you come?"
She answers, "Yes."

Duke: You little rascal, you had to come, had to come, had
          to come,
          You little rascal, you had to come, ranson, transon,
          ti-e-i-oh.

FORMATION: Six children stand in line and one child is chosen
to be the duke. The duke goes back from the line, about ten
feet. The game can be played by girls with the girls taking turns
being the duke.

ACTION: As the duke sings, he advances and retreats. The others
sing as they advance and retreat. When all verses have been sung
the duke takes his place in line, and his partner becomes the
duke. This procedure continues until all have had a chance to
be the duke. "Any number may play, but I find six the best
number. When there are as many as thirteen or fifteen, I divide
them seven and six, all in line, two groups a few feet apart, and
that way two groups are singing and playing at the same time."

SOURCE: Mrs. Edith Mescher, Grantsburg, Illinois, November,
1946.

GENTLEMEN FROM SPAIN

Here comes one gen-tle-man just from Spain, come to court your daugh-ter Jane. My daugh-ter Jane is much too young, to be con-trolled by an-y one.

Gentleman: Here comes one gentleman just from Spain,
Come to court your daughter, Jane.

Mother: My daughter, Jane, is much too young,
To be controlled by anyone.

Gentleman: Let her be old, let her be young,
It is my duty and it must be done.

Mother: Stand back, stand back, you sassy one,
And choose the fairest in the land.

Gentleman: The fairest one that I can see,
Will be Miss . . . ., come walk with me.

Mother and others: Good-by Miss . . . ., good-by, good-by,
Look in your pocket, you'll find a gold locket.

NOTE: This version of the game is designed to be played by girls, with one girl acting the part of the first gentleman. As each girl is chosen, she becomes a gentleman.

FORMATION: All players line up on one side except one who is the first "Gentleman." He faces all the players on the other side. One of the players in line is the mother.

ACTION: The gentleman and the mother sing the verses alternately, after which the gentleman chooses one to go with him. That one now becomes another gentleman, and the singing starts over, "Here come two gentlemen, etc." The game continues until all but one have gone to the gentleman's side. The remaining one becomes the new "gentleman," and a new mother is chosen.

SOURCE: Mrs. Maggie G. Branch, Mounds, Illinois.

DRAW A BUCKET OF WATER

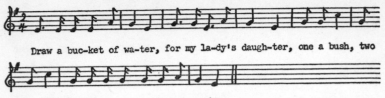

Draw a buc-ket of wa-ter, for my la-dy's daugh-ter, one a bush, two
a bush, let a lit-tle la-dy get un-der.

FORMATION: Four children form a single circle, (1) boy, (2) girl, (3) boy, (4) girl, or four girls, or four boys. The children standing opposite to each other join both hands straight across forming a square of four arms and hands.

ACTION: On the first beat of each measure number 1 and number 2 pull, as number 3 and number 4 push; on the second beat of each measure, the action is reversed. At the end of the verse, number 1 and number 3 raise the joined right hand of number 1 and left hand of number 3 over the head of number 2. The verse is sung four times, and arms are raised over each child in turn, so as to form a tight circle with arms around each child. Now the four children in this tight circle jump up and down as they circle to the left, and chant three times, "Jump, jump, sugar lump, you'll all jump down." It is expected that the children will fall down before they reach the end of the chant.

SOURCE: Mrs. Leona Stunkel, Edwardsville, Illinois.

GOING DOWN TO NEW ORLEANS

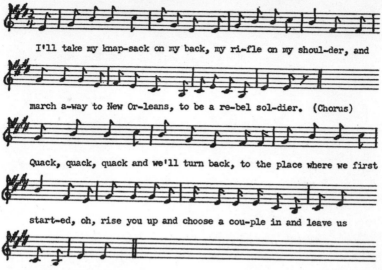

I'll take my knap-sack on my back, my ri-fle on my shoul-der, and

march a-way to New Or-leans, to be a re-bel sol-dier. (Chorus)

Quack, quack, quack and we'll turn back, to the place where we first

start-ed, oh, rise you up and choose a cou-ple in and leave us

bro-ken heart-ed.

FORMATION: Couples are seated side by side in two rows of chairs placed back to back in the center of the room. One extra couple, with hands joined behind their backs in skating position, prepare to march around the row of seated couples.

ACTION: Everyone sings as standing couple marches around. On the words, "We'll turn back," the marching couple reverses direction and continues marching. The reverse is done by turning away from each other, keeping hold of hands.

On the words, "Rise you up," every seated couple must change seats, and in the scramble the marching couple gets a seat. The couple left without a seat marches around as the game is repeated. In the scramble for seats, couples must not become separated. The lady must be seated to the right of her partner.

SOURCE: Mrs. Edith Travis Mescher, Grantsburg, Illinois, 1946.

GRANDMA GRAY

(Words to the game are spoken.)

Children: Grandma Gray, may I go out to play?

Grandma: No, tomorrow is your sister's wedding day; you'll get your dress dirty.

Children: I'm going anyhow.

Grandma: Children.

Children: We don't hear you.

Grandma: Children!

Children: We don't hear you.

Grandma: I'll send my dog after you.

Children: We don't hear you.

Grandma: I'll send my cat after you.

Children: We don't hear you.

Grandma: I'll send my switch after you.

Children: We don't hear you.

Grandma: I'll send myself after you.

FORMATION: Any number of players. All in a group anywhere.

ACTION: One player is chosen "grandma." The rest are the children. They remain in a group until they say, "I'm going anyhow," then the children run off (scatter). When grandma says, "I'll send myself after you," she runs to catch the children. The one caught is grandma for the next game. Any number of animals may be named in the phrase—I'll send my cow after you, to add variety; pony, chicken, rabbit, and so on.

SOURCE: Pattie Cole, Cairo, Illinois, 1947, and Frances Pond, Cairo, Illinois.

VARIATION FOR GRANDMA GRAY

When grandma sends the switch for the children, they all gather around her. Each child is asked in turn where he has been and how much money he made. The children reply five cents, ten cents, or any amount. The money is to be put on a shelf. Grandma says to each child, "If I fall down and break my neck, will you be glad or sorry?" If a child says, "Sorry," it's all right, but if a child says, "Glad," grandma runs after him, and if he is caught, he receives several spanks. The last child caught is grandma for the next game.

SOURCE: Stevetta A. Harrell, Villa Ridge, Illinois, 1947.

HERE SITS A YOUNG MAN

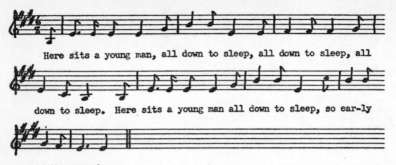

Here sits a young man, all down to sleep, all down to sleep, all down to sleep. Here sits a young man all down to sleep, so ear-ly in the morn-ing.

2. He wants a young lady to keep him awake,
To keep him awake, to keep him awake,
He wants a young lady to keep him awake,
So early in the morning.

3. Just write her name down and send it to me,
And send it to me, and send it to me,
Just write her name down and send it to me,
So early in the morning.

4. Her name it is written, you'll all hear it called,
You'll all hear it called, you'll all hear it called,
Her name it is written you'll all hear it called,
So early in the morning.

5. Miss Jennie Johnson, her name it is called,
Her name it is called, her name it is called,
Miss Jennie Johnson, her name it is called,
So early in the morning.

6. So rise you up now and bring her to me,
Bring her to me, bring her to me,
So rise you up now and bring her to me,
So early in the morning.

FORMATION: A young man is seated on a chair in the center of the room; he pretends to be asleep. One couple is chosen to begin the marching. Other couples are standing or seated nearby.

ACTION: Verses 1 and 2. One couple marches around the young man in the chair as all sing.

Verse 3. At the beginning of this verse, the young lady of the marching couple stoops down and the sleeper whispers in her ear the name of some young lady in the room.

Verse 4. The couple continues marching.

Verse 5. The couple continues marching. The name of the young lady named by the sleeper is sung instead of "Miss Jennie Johnson."

Verse 6. The marching couple goes to the lady chosen and brings her to the chair. She takes the place of the young man.
As the game is repeated, the verses are changed so as to apply to the young lady. The young man marches behind the couple; he is joined by the lady of his choice as the game is repeated the third time.

SOURCE: Robert Wilson, Dalgren, Illinois, 1938.

LEAD UP TWO

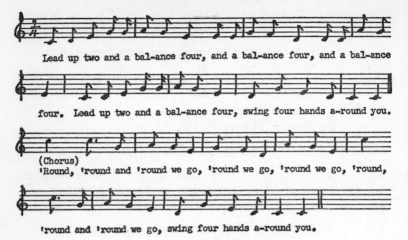

Lead up two and a bal-ance four, and a bal-ance four, and a bal-ance

four. Lead up two and a bal-ance four, swing four hands a-round you.

(Chorus)
'Round, 'round and 'round we go, 'round we go, 'round we go, 'round,

'round and 'round we go, swing four hands a-round you.

2. Lady pass through with a do-si-do,
   And a do-si-do, and a do-si-do,
   Lady pass through with a do-si-do,
   Swing four hands around you.

FORMATION: Two couples stand in a circle with hands joined.

ACTION: Verse 1. All take four steps toward the center on the first line, four steps backward on the second line, four steps forward on the third line, and four steps backward on the fourth line. (These four steps must be very short; as additional couples are brought into the game four full steps can be taken.)

Chorus. All join hands and circle to the left.

Verse 2. All the gentlemen execute the Allemande Left with the lady on the left, an Allemande Right with their partners, an Allemande Left with the lady on the left, and an Allemande Right with their partner.

Chorus. All join hands and circle to the left.

Before the game is repeated, a third couple is invited into the circle and at each repetition of the game, an additional couple is invited to join the circle. This game was used as an "icebreaker." As the game is repeated the numbers are changed to match the number of players in the game. For the first repetition of the game the first verse is as follows:

> Lead up three and a balance six,
> And a balance six, and a balance six,
> Lead up three and a balance six,
> Swing six hands around you.

SOURCE: Joe Simmons, Vienna, Illinois, 1940.

OLD BLOODY TOM

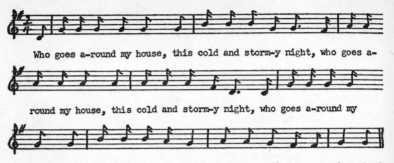

Who goes a-round my house, this cold and storm-y night, who goes a-

round my house, this cold and storm-y night, who goes a-round my

house, this cold and storm-y night, while my chil-dren are sleep-ing?

Mother:

1. Who goes around my house this cold and stormy night?
   Who goes around my house this cold and stormy night?
   Who goes around my house this cold and stormy night,
   While my children are sleeping?

Tom:

2. Old Bloody Tom—this cold and stormy night.
   Old Bloody Tom—this cold and stormy night.
   Old Bloody Tom—this cold and stormy night,
   While your children are sleeping.

Mother:

3. Oh, what do you want this cold and stormy night?
   Oh, what do you want this cold and stormy night?
   Oh, what do you want this cold and stormy night,
   While my children are sleeping.

Tom:

4. I want one of your children so bright.
   I want one of your children so bright.
   I want one of your children so bright,
   While your children are sleeping.

Mother:

5. Take the meanest and leave the best.
    Take the meanest and leave the best.
    And never come back to bother the rest,
    While my children are sleeping.

Tom:

6. I'll take the meanest and leave the best.
    I'll take the meanest and leave the best.
    And never come back to bother the rest,
    While your children are sleeping.

RULES FOR PLAYING: "Children holding hands form a circle and walk around the one in the center, chosen as the mother. Mother sings first line alone. All the children and mother sing, together, lines 2 and 3. Mother sings last line of each verse alone, as the children stop circling around mother and put their hands over their eyes.

"While Tom is singing, the children stand still just holding hands. Tom sings in a very gruff voice. On the last verse as the mother sings, mother and children cover eyes on the word 'Sleeping.' Tom sings his last verse while they are in this position. When Tom finishes singing, he grabs some child and runs anticlockwise around the circle, holding hands of child chosen. He must not turn loose the hand of the child. Mother runs out of circle at place where the child was taken; she must not cut through or go back to meet him. If she catches up with Tom and the child, she gets to take the child inside the circle with her and keep it. If Tom gets the child away, he takes it to his hide-out, and the game goes on until all the children have been taken or until the children get tired or the bell rings for 'books.' "

SOURCE: Stella Lumsden, Zeigler, Illinois.

THIMBLE GAME

Leader: Thimble moving?

All: Yes, yes.

Leader: Keep it moving.

All: Yes, yes.

Leader: Who's got the thimble?

All: I don't know.

Leader: Thimble moving?

All: Yes, yes.

Leader: Rise, old thimble, rise.

DIRECTIONS: A leader is chosen. All other players sit on the floor or stand in a circle. A thimble is passed quickly from one to another in any direction.

The dialogue is chanted in rhythm, two beats to each line, except the last which has one extra beat on the last word.

As the leader says, "Rise, old thimble, rise," the one who has the thimble must go to the center of the circle with the leader.

The game is played until most of the players have been caught.

SOURCE: G. Holmes, Sparta, Illinois.